*D*o you know what you are?
You are a marvel. You are unique.
In all the years that have passed,
there has never been another child like you.

Pablo Casals (1876–1973)

My *Thoughts* *with* *Love*

A Parent's Keepsake Journal

ANNE GEDDES

My Thoughts with Love

from

....

Date

*I*t was the Rainbow gave thee birth,
  And left thee all her lovely hues.

William Henry Davies (1871–1940)

Date

Date

𝒜 new baby is like the beginning
of all things – wonder, hope, a dream of possibilities.

Eda J. Leshan (1922–)

Date

Date ....

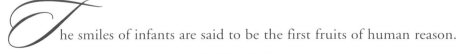

The smiles of infants are said to be the first fruits of human reason.

Rev. Henry N. Hudson

Date

Date

Date ....

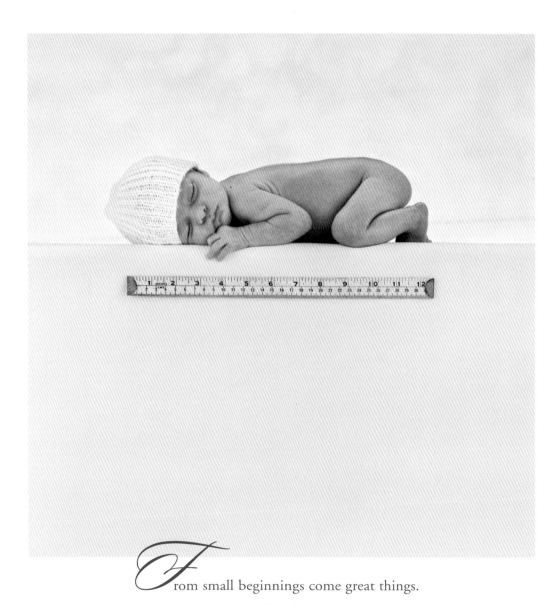

From small beginnings come great things.

Proverb

Date ....

Date ....

Date

Date

A mother understands what a child does not say.

Proverb

Date

Date

Date

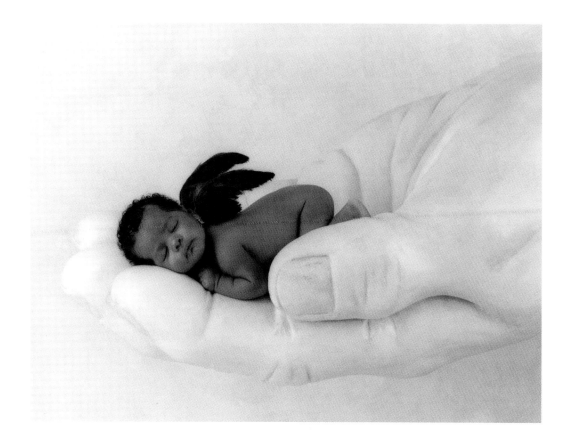

*I*t lay upon its mother's breast, a thing
Bright as a dewdrop when it first descends,
Or as the plumage of an angel's wing,
Where every tint of rainbow beauty blends.

Amelia Welby (1821–1852)

Date

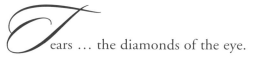

Tears … the diamonds of the eye.

Rev. Dr. Davies

Date

Date

Each day I love you more …
today, more than yesterday …
and less than tomorrow.

Rosemonde Gérard

Date

Date

Date

When you havva no babies –
you havva nothing.

Italian immigrant woman

Date

Date

Date

Date ....

I have spread my dreams under your feet;
Tread softly because you tread on my dreams.

W. B. Yeats (1865–1939)

Date

Date

Date

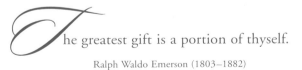he greatest gift is a portion of thyself.

Ralph Waldo Emerson (1803–1882)

Date

Date

Date

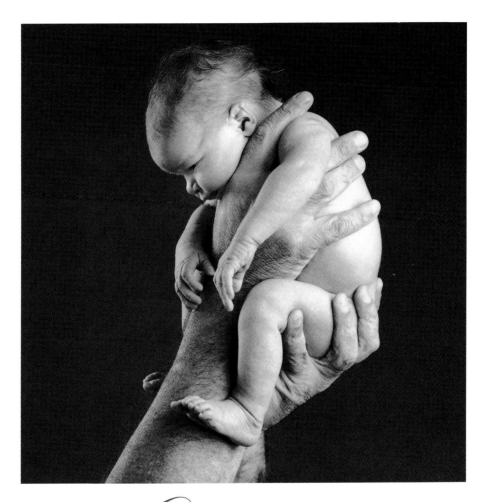

O wonderful, wonderful,
and most wonderful wonderful!
and yet again wonderful.

William Shakespeare (1564–1616)

Date

Date

Date ....

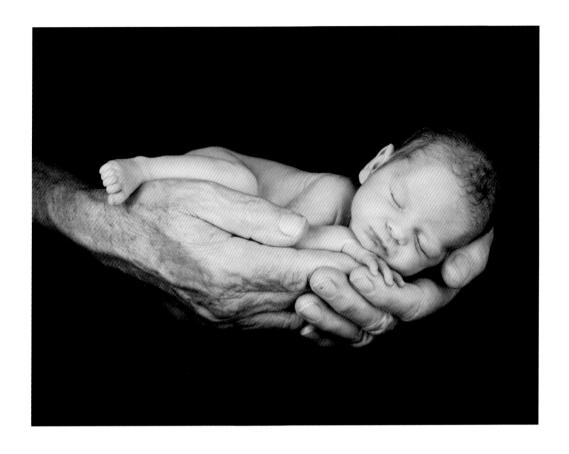

*W*e can do no great things –
only small things with great love.

Mother Teresa (1910–1997)

Date

Date

Date

*T*here are only two lasting bequests
we can hope to give our children.
One of these is roots; the other, wings.

Cecilia Lasbury

Date

Date

The very pink of perfection.

Oliver Goldsmith (1728–1774)

ANNE GEDDES ™

ISBN 0-8362-1915-5

© Anne Geddes 1999

Published in 1999 by Photogenique Publishers
(a division of Hodder Moa Beckett)
Studio 3.16, Axis Building, 1 Cleveland Road, Parnell
Auckland, New Zealand

First Canadian edition published in 1999 by Andrews McMeel Publishing,
4520 Main Street, Kansas City, MO 64111-7701

Designed by Lucy Richardson
Produced by Kel Geddes
Color separations by MH Group

Printed by Midas Printing Limited, Hong Kong